Tag-a-Long!

A story about a surprisingly, real-life friendship
between a boy and a duckling named Tag-a-long.

Author, Karen A. Reid
Illustrated by Mary McLeod

Florina,
You are
beautiful!!!

Karen Reid

Davey wanted to try his luck at winning a baby duck at the county fair. "Yeah, I won he shouted!" The man placed the duckling in a cardboard box and handed it to Davey. The little boy was so excited that he ran to show his mom what he had won.

Davey will have many lessons in being responsible as he cares for this duckling, thought his mother.

Davey stroked the soft yellow feathers, and took the duck inside the house and wrapped it in a blanket. Davey wondered if his new duckling would like his two older, white ducks in his backyard.

The duckling followed Davey everywhere he went in the house. Davey named the new duckling, Tag-a-long!

Tag-a-long grew to like his new friend and Davey loved playing with his baby duckling every day.

Davey showed Tag-a-long how to ride on his toy train. Tag-a-long sat on the flatbed car and rode around and around on the track. Davey pretended that he was the engineer and that Tag-a-long was the conductor, calling out the stops along the route.

Tag-a-long loved to climb up into Davey's big, red, cattle truck too!
Davey raced the truck up and down the hallway just like truckers
do on the highway.

Tag-a-long was growing bigger and bigger and he was moved outside. Davey's two older, white ducks named Henry and Henrietta welcomed the new duckling.

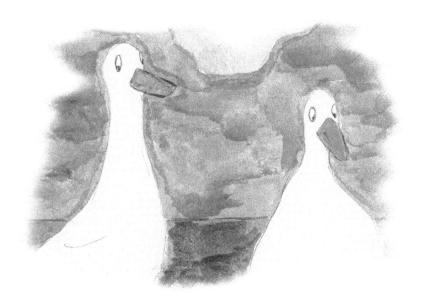

The old dog house in the back yard is where Tag-a-long, Henry and Henrietta slept at night. Davey cared for Tag-a-long just like moms care for their babies. He fed Tag-a-long and the older ducks cornmeal and green vegetables.

When Davey's family went to the store, Tag-a-long decided that he wanted to ride in the car too.

Tag-a-long perched himself on the back of the front seat in the big green and white family car.

His favorite outing was to the lake. Kids were sitting with their feet in the sand. So Tag-a-long waddled over and tried to nibble at their toes. The children laughed! They knew that Tag-a-long would not hurt them.

At home, Tag-a-long had fun swinging on
the swing set next to Davey. They talked
and sang songs while watching and
listening to birds in the garden.
There are many beautiful things in this
world thought Tag-a-long.

One day Davey's mother caught Tag-a-long, Henry and Henrietta eating the fresh buds off of her Dahlia plants. She yelled, "Stop!" Davey's mother wasn't upset for very long as she remembered how helpful the ducks were as they often ate bugs and slugs in the garden. It's important to help others when we can thought Tag-a-long!

Later that summer, Davey's Dad came home from work saying that the family needed to move to another city for Dad's new job. Ducks were not allowed in the new neighborhood.

Davey and his mom found a new home for Tag-a-long, Henry and Henrietta to the zoo.

Davey shouted, "I hope you like your new home Tag-a-long!"

"I'll try, thought Tag-a-long as he waddled away.

Sometimes we are sad when we have to leave our friends or family.

Davey knew that the ducks would be well taken care of with new friends at the zoo.

Davey will always be happy when thinking about his special friend, Tag-a-long.

Throughout life we all are called
upon to say a sorrowful goodbye to someone we love.
Thank goodness memories of that special someone are held in our
warm heart forever, bringing us ongoing joy throughout the years!

Karen's career in education spans over four decades. As Educators, parents and caregivers, we are often called upon to listen to and support young people who are experiencing sadness due to great loss. This story was written as a tribute to her husband, David as he reflected on his childhood memories of his pet duckling. For those who are saddened by the loss of a special pet, a friend or a loved one, or for those longing for a loved one to return home, may they find comfort in this real life, boyhood story.

Dr. Reid, her husband and two grown children live in the greater Seattle area.

CPSIA information can be obtained
at www.ICGtesting.com
Printed in the USA
BVHW021529050422
633383BV00002B/9